REACH

© Copyright 2017 by Shane Stanford. All Rights Reserved.

Published by **MAKING LIFE MATTER, LLC**

shanestanfordmlm.com

REACH
SHANE STANFORD

MAKING LIFE MATTER

OUR MISSION AND VALUES

Christ Church exists to glorify God as we Make, Mature and Mobilize Disciples of Jesus Christ by Loving Jesus and Loving Like Jesus in the world.

We commit ourselves to the following values as described in Acts 2:42-47:

Worship: *Glorifying God in all things*

Care: *Doing life together*

Share: *Practicing generosity*

Grow: *Making disciples who make disciples*

Serve: *Being the hands and feet of Jesus*

WHAT IS REACH?

OUR PURPOSE AND OBJECTIVES

Purpose: What does it mean for the body of Christ to REACH the world for Jesus—to glorify God as we *Make, Mature and Mobilize Disciples... by loving Jesus and loving like Jesus in the world?*

Our objective through the REACH program is to engage Scripture and the Holy Spirit in answering this question that we might boldly, faithfully and graciously impact our relationships, community and world for the Good News of the Gospel.

HOW DOES THE REACH STUDY GUIDE WORK?

THE WEEKLY STUDY FRAMEWORK

1. **SCRIPTURE:** All Scriptures are available in the booklet using the Common English Bible.

2. **DAILY DEVOTIONAL SUGGESTIONS:** There is a seven-day Scripture reading plan available for each week's lesson.

3. **REFLECTION AND STUDY QUESTIONS:** Each week, we will ask four types of questions from our study together:

    REACHING UP: What does God say through God's Word about REACHing the world with the hope of Christ? (Listening)
    Includes: Scripture focus and study questions

REACHING IN: What does it mean for us to place God's Word into our personal and communal spiritual lives? (Understanding)

Includes: Personal study narrative and focus questions

REACHING DOWN: What and how do we need to prepare for responding to God's Word in the world? (Preparing)

Includes: Checklist for next steps for both personal and community preparedness

REACHING OUT: What is the challenge and objective as we reach beyond the walls with God's Word for the world? (Responding)

Includes: Challenge for the week in regard to that week's focus area, a prayer focus, a suggested prayer, a #hashtag focus and for further reading suggestion

4. **LIFE TIPS:** Dr. Pokey Stanford provides study and response tips for teachers and leaders at the end of each week's lesson.

5. **NEXT STEPS:** Where do we go from here? How do we respond to what God has taught and shown us through His Word? These steps allow us to not only respond but to also do so with strategic intention.

6. **RESPONSE/SOCIAL MEDIA:** A social media prompt will be given to encourage everyone on the journey to share his or her thoughts, suggestions and opinions.

WEEK-BY-WEEK STUDY OUTLINE:

WEEK ONE: REJOICE—We begin our response to God's Word pointing our lives back to God for worship and study.

Primary Scripture: Philippians 4:4-7

4 Be glad in the Lord always! Again I say, be glad! 5 Let your gentleness show in your treatment of all people. The Lord is near. 6 Don't be anxious about anything; rather, bring up all of your requests to God in your prayers and petitions, along with giving thanks. 7 Then the peace of God that exceeds all understanding will keep your hearts and minds safe in Christ Jesus.

WEEK TWO: EQUIP—We must provide the tools and opportunities to make, mature and mobilize disciples for Jesus Christ.

Primary Scripture: Ephesians 4:12-16

12 His purpose was to equip God's people for the work of serving and building up the body of Christ 13 until we all reach the unity of faith and knowledge of God's Son. God's goal is for us to become mature adults—to be fully grown, measured by the standard of the fullness of Christ. 14 As a result, we aren't supposed to be infants any longer who can be tossed and blown around by every wind that comes from teaching with deceitful scheming and the tricks people play to deliberately mislead others. 15 Instead, by speaking the truth with love, let's grow in every way into Christ, 16 who is the head. The whole body grows from him, as it is joined and held together by all the supporting ligaments. The body makes itself grow in that it builds itself up with love as each one does its part.

WEEK THREE: ADVANCE—We must gather the resources, skills and person power to move God's plan from words to action.
Primary Scripture: Matthew 28:16-20

16 Now the eleven disciples went to Galilee, to the mountain to which Jesus had directed them. 17 And when they saw him they worshiped him, but some doubted. 18 And Jesus came and said to them, "All authority in heaven and on earth has been given to me. 19 Go therefore and make disciples of all nations, baptizing them in[b] the name of the Father and of the Son and of the Holy Spirit, 20 teaching them to observe all that I have commanded you. And behold, I am with you always, to the end of the age."

WEEK FOUR: COMMIT—We must raise the bar for community and mutual accountability to live and work as the body of Christ together.

Primary Scripture: Acts 2:42-47

42 The believers devoted themselves to the apostles' teaching, to the community, to their shared meals, and to their prayers. 43 A sense of awe came over everyone. God performed many wonders and signs through the apostles. 44 All the believers were united and shared everything. 45 They would sell pieces of property and possessions and distribute the proceeds to everyone who needed them. 46 Every day, they met together in the temple and ate in their homes. They shared food with gladness and simplicity. 47 They praised God and demonstrated God's goodness to everyone. The Lord added daily to the community those who were being saved.

WEEK FIVE: HEAL—We must seek healing in all that we are and do as the body of Christ as we REACH the world for Jesus.
Primary Scriptures: Matthew 8:16-17 & Matthew 9:35

16 That evening people brought to Jesus many who were demon-possessed. He threw the spirits out with just a word. He healed everyone who was sick. 17 This happened so that what Isaiah the prophet said would be fulfilled: He is the one who took our illnesses and carried away our diseases.
(Matthew 8:16-17)

35 Jesus traveled among all the cities and villages, teaching in their synagogues, announcing the good news of the kingdom, and healing every disease and every sickness. (Matthew 9:35)

OUR RESPONSE FOR 2018 AND BEYOND

Of course, one of our major reasons for REACH 2018 is for Christ Church to prepare, engage and respond to God's plan for our congregation in 2018 and beyond. This includes our commitment to the following:

1. Worshipping regularly at Christ Church via one of our weekend worship services or our Online Campus
2. Doing Life Together in a small group for fellowship, study and serving—i.e., Sunday school, etc.
3. Sharing our resources to support the financial and fiscal life of the body of Christ—working toward at least a tithe of our income or more
4. Committing us to a deeper walk in God's Word for growing our personal story and then sharing that Great Story with others along our journey
5. Serving as the 'hands and feet' of Jesus Christ in the world— whether experienced *across the street or around the world*

OUR STEWARDSHIP COVENANT

Although we manage our strategic priorities according to the Five Values of Christ Church, our 2018 Ministry Operations Plan is divided according to the following estimated fiscal areas:

1. SHARE	$ 2,600,000
2. CARE	$ 600,000
3. GROW	$ 1,175,000
4. WORSHIP	$ 825,000
5. SERVE	$ 2,470,000
Total Ministry Operations:	$ 7,670,000

The above estimates are proposals based on a 3-5 percent increase in the ministry operations plan from 2017. These are estimates only.

Take time to begin our journey together by reading John Wesley's *Covenant Prayer*. Normally prayed at New Year's, this prayer is about new beginnings and about REACHING beyond our normal limits to achieve great things for God and God's Kingdom.

OUR COVENANT PRAYER FOR CHRIST CHURCH

By John Wesley

I am no longer my own, but yours.

Put me to what you will, rank me with whom you will;

put me to doing, put me to suffering;

let me be employed for you, or laid aside for you,

exalted for you, or brought low for you;

let me be full,

let me be empty,

let me have all things,

let me have nothing:

I freely and wholeheartedly yield all things

to your pleasure and disposal.

And now, glorious and blessed God,

Father, Son and Holy Spirit,

you are mine and I am yours. So be it.

And the covenant now made on earth, let it be ratified in heaven.

Amen.

WEEK ONE: REJOICE

We **REACH to the world** by pointing our lives back to God for worship and study.

PRIMARY SCRIPTURE: PHILIPPIANS 4:4-7

Please take time to read the following Scripture and point your heart and soul back to God that you may hear God's Word and encouragement this week.

4 Be glad in the Lord always! Again I say, be glad! 5 Let your gentleness show in your treatment of all people. The Lord is near. 6 Don't be anxious about anything; rather, bring up all of your requests to God in your prayers and petitions, along with giving thanks. 7 Then the peace of God that exceeds all understanding will keep your hearts and minds safe in Christ Jesus.

SERMON AND WORSHIP OUTLINE NOTES

Worship Songs or Hymns that Inspired Me:
_____

The Setting and Other Scriptures:
_____

The Primary Message:
_____

Sermon Outlines and Notes:
_____
_____
_____
_____
_____
_____
_____
_____
_____
_____

What Did the Holy Spirit Say to Me Today?

_____

_____

_____

_____

_____

SEVEN-DAY READING PLAN

Sunday	Philippians 4:4-7
Monday	Psalm 8:1
Tuesday	John 4:21-24
Wednesday	James 4:8
Thursday	Romans 12:1-2
Friday	Galatians 2: 20
Saturday	Psalm 59:16

REFLECTION AND STUDY QUESTIONS

Each week, we will ask four types of questions from our study together of the Scripture lesson:

A. **REACHING UP:** What does God say through God's Word about REACHing the world with the hope of Christ? (Listening) Read Philippians 4:4-7 once again.

What does it mean for 'our gentleness to show in our treatment of all people'? How does our treatment of others bring glory to God and rejoice in His will? How do our anxieties or feelings of peace affect our ability to worship and rejoice in Christ?

Notes:

_____

_____

_____

_____

B. **REACHING IN:** What does it mean for us to place God's Word as a means for rejoicing and worship into our personal and communal spiritual lives? (Understanding)

What do our rejoicing lives look like to the outside world? When people see us, do they want to rejoice or recoil at faith?

How often do you worship and take time to rejoice during the week? Explain.

Notes:
_____
_____
_____
_____
_____

C. **REACHING DOWN:** What and how do we need to prepare for responding to God's Word in the world through worship and as worshippers? (Preparing)

What is one commitment you could make to God right now that would change your worship life immediately? What would such a commitment say to God? To others?

Do a 'Scripture mine' whereby you list 15-20 Scriptures about worship and rejoicing in God's presence. How would using these Scriptures for the next five weeks reshape your worship life? Keep a journal and make notes.

Notes:

_____

_____

_____

_____

_____

D. REACHING OUT: What are the challenge and objective as we reach beyond the walls with God's Word for the world? (Responding)

Take time to read Richard Foster's *Celebration of Discipline*. What forms of the spiritual disciplines do you practice—i.e., prayer, fasting, forgiveness, etc.?

Name one or two people you could reach out to in order to invite them to worship or at least ask for the forgiveness **you need** to move forward in your own worship.

Notes:

_____

_____

_____

_____

_____

_____

LIFE & STUDY TIPS
by Dr. Pokey Stanford

As a teacher or leader of a small group, reflect on how your own personal worship life affects how you lead and teach others. How does your rejoicing (or lack thereof) affect your ability to share the Good News?

A joyful heart is half the journey for those who teach and lead. Take a moment to list all of the people in the classes you teach or lead. Now, take time to pray for them by name. They don't have to be long, complex prayers—just simple petitions of God for their clarity, connection and commitment to God and God's people. This simple tool will not only draw you closer to each other, but will also set a foundation for your class to grow closer to God.

_____

_____

_____

_____

NEXT STEPS

We too often pass by the places, people and moments where rejoicing could have its greatest effect. Be intentional to write in your journal each day all of the opportunities the Holy Spirit provides for you to rejoice. In fact, call the list the 'Rejoicing List'—you may want to keep it going after the REACH campaign is finished. Maybe you will be surprised at how many people need your rejoicing—and how that rejoicing can change the dynamic for so many other areas of our walk in the world.

For those of you who need tangible signs, gather rocks, coins or a special marker that you don't mind giving away. Every place you go this week that needs your rejoicing, simply leave that marker behind. Don't make a scene; just leave it as a reminder between God and you, that this place is not forgotten.

RESPONSE/SOCIAL MEDIA

Make a list of the tweets, posts or discussions you saw this week on social media about rejoicing and worship that engaged your thoughts and spirit.

Any #hashtags catch your eye?

Any 'tweets of wisdom' you plan to share?

WEEK TWO: EQUIP

We **REACH to the world** by providing the tools and opportunities to make, mature and mobilize disciples for Jesus Christ.

PRIMARY SCRIPTURE: EPHESIANS 4:12-16

Please take time to read the following Scripture and point your heart and soul back to God that you may hear God's Word and equip yourself and others to live 'on mission' for Christ this week.

12 His purpose was to equip God's people for the work of serving and building up the body of Christ 13 until we all reach the unity of faith and knowledge of God's Son. God's goal is for us to become mature adults—to be fully grown, measured by the standard of the fullness of Christ. 14 As a result, we aren't supposed to be infants any longer who can be tossed and blown around by every wind that comes from teaching with deceitful scheming and the tricks people play to deliberately mislead others. 15 Instead, by speaking the truth with love, let's grow in every way into Christ, 16 who is the head. The whole body grows from him, as it is joined and held together by all the supporting ligaments. The body makes itself grow in that it builds itself up with love as each one does its part.

SERMON AND WORSHIP OUTLINE NOTES

Worship Songs or Hymns that Inspired Me:
_____

The Setting:
_____

The Primary Message:
_____

Sermon Outlines and Notes:
_____
_____
_____
_____
_____

What Did the Holy Spirit Say to Me Today?

_____

_____

_____

SEVEN-DAY READING PLAN

Sunday	Ephesians 4:12-16
Monday	Isaiah 50:4-7
Tuesday	Matthew 12:18
Wednesday	Luke 4:18-19
Thursday	John 3:34
Friday	Acts 10:38
Saturday	Matthew 4:19

REFLECTION AND STUDY QUESTIONS

Each week, we will ask four types of questions from our study together of the Scripture lesson:

A. **REACHING UP**: What does God say through God's Word about REACHing the world with the hope of Christ? (Listening) Read Ephesians 4:12-16.

What does it mean for us to become 'mature adults' who reach the 'fullness of Christ'? How does equipping others (and thus being equipped ourselves) help us along this journey?

Notes:

_____

_____

_____

_____

_____

B. **REACHING IN:** What does it mean for us to place God's Word as a means for equipping ourselves and others for serving in the body of Christ deep in our personal and communal spiritual lives? (Understanding)

How would the world define what it means to equip? Are there differences between the world's definition and the Word's?

What has to 'go' in your life in order for you to be a faithful 'equipper' for the body of Christ? Therefore, with what gifts do you need to be equipped in order to become all that God has in store?

Notes:

_____

_____

_____

_____

_____

C. **REACHING DOWN:** What and how do we need to prepare for responding to God's Word in the world through being equipped and becoming equippers for walking with Christ? (Preparing)

What is one commitment you could make to God right now that would change the way you do life immediately? What would such a commitment say to God? To others?

Do a 'Scripture mine' whereby you list 15-20 Scriptures about being equipped with the spiritual gifts of God. How would using these Scriptures for the next five weeks reshape your study, fellowship and serving life? Keep a journal and make notes.

Notes:

_____

_____

_____

_____

_____

D. REACHING OUT: What are the challenge and objective as we reach beyond the walls with God's Word for the world? (Responding)

Take time to read Shane Stanford's *You Can't Do Everything... So Do Something*. List the 'somethings' you can do today that would make a difference for Christ.

Name one or two people you could reach out to in order to pray for the work of God in their lives. How could others pray for you today? Ask someone to pray specifically for you.

Notes:

_____

_____

_____

_____

_____

_____

_____

LIFE & STUDY TIPS

by Dr. Pokey Stanford

As a teacher or leader in the body of Christ, we are called to use our spiritual gifts and to equip others to do the same. God moves powerfully when we can bring our gifts, skills and passions to respond to the brokenness in the world. Not sure what your gifts, skills and passions are? Contact the Serving and Outreach office at Christ Church, (901) 683-3521.

NEXT STEPS

Make a list of your top three spiritual gifts. How can you use them today? Take some time to do some intentional act or response using each of your spiritual gifts today.

Now, list these responses in your journal or sermon notes above. As the week closes, review how each of these gifts played out for service in the Kingdom. What one of these gifts or actions would you keep day-to-day from that point on?

RESPONSE/SOCIAL MEDIA

Make a list of the tweets, posts or discussions you saw this week on social media about equipping and using our spiritual gifts that engaged your thoughts and spirit.

Any #hashtags catch your eye?

Any 'tweets of wisdom' you plan to share?

WEEK THREE: ADVANCE

We REACH to the world by gathering the resources, skills and person power to move God's plan from words to action.

PRIMARY SCRIPTURE: MATTHEW 28:16-20

Please take time to read the following Scripture and point your heart and soul back to God that you may hear God's Word and advance the Kingdom for Christ this week.

16 Now the eleven disciples went to Galilee, to the mountain to which Jesus had directed them. 17 And when they saw him they worshiped him, but some doubted. 18 And Jesus came and said to them, "All authority in heaven and on earth has been given to me. 19 Go therefore and make disciples of all nations, baptizing them in[b] the name of the Father and of the Son and of the Holy Spirit, 20 teaching them to observe all that I have commanded you. And behold, I am with you always, to the end of the age."

SERMON AND WORSHIP OUTLINE NOTES

Worship Songs or Hymns that Inspired Me:
_____

The Setting:
_____

The Primary Message:
_____

Sermon Outlines and Notes:
_____
_____
_____
_____
_____

What Did the Holy Spirit Say to Me Today?
_____
_____
_____
_____

SEVEN-DAY READING PLAN

Sunday	Matthew 28:16-20
Monday	Romans 10:10-17
Tuesday	Matthew 9:37-38
Wednesday	1 Corinthians 9:22
Thursday	1 Peter 3:15
Friday	Colossians 4:2-6
Saturday	1 Corinthians 1:17

REFLECTION AND STUDY QUESTIONS

Each week, we will ask four types of questions from our study together of the Scripture lesson:

A. **REACHING UP**: What does God say through God's Word about REACHing the world with the hope of Christ? (Listening) Read Matthew 28:16-20.

What does it mean in the passage to 'go'? How does our 'going' itself represent part of our spiritual obedience? Where are places that Jesus went and then also sent His disciples during His earthly ministry?

Define what Jesus means by 'baptize' and 'teach' whenever we are sent into the world. What does it mean for Jesus to 'be with us until the end of the age'?

Notes:

_____

_____

_____

_____

_____

B. REACHING IN: What does it mean for us to live out God's Word as a means for sharing the Good News of Jesus Christ in our personal relationships? (Understanding)

How would the world define a 'witness' or the 'act of witnessing'? Think of a court of law. What is a witness' responsibility? Who holds the witness accountable?

Where are the places you go in this world? How can you share your faith through your example and words in these places and relationships? What needs to be removed or changed in your life (or daily routine) to become better at being sent into the world?

What qualifications must one have in order to teach the Word of God to those whom we are sent?

Notes:

_____

_____

_____

_____

_____

C. **REACHING DOWN**: What should your devotional/study life look like to faithfully share your witness in Christ? Any changes that might be helpful in becoming more like Christ as you share the Good News? Do any of your relationships, current habits or patterns, or 'tender' places in life need to change or be adjusted before you 'walk back into the world as a witness for Jesus'? (Preparing)

What is one commitment you could make to God right now that would change the way you do life immediately? What would such a commitment say to God? To others?

Do a 'Scripture mine' whereby you list 15-20 Scriptures about witnessing and sharing the Good News of Jesus Christ. How would using these Scriptures for the next five weeks reshape your study, fellowship and serving life? Keep a journal and make notes.

Notes:

_____

_____

_____

_____

_____

D. **REACHING OUT**: What are the challenge and objective as we reach beyond the walls with God's Word for the world? (Responding)

Take time to read *Unlearning Church* by Michael Slaughter.

Name one or two people you could reach out to in order to pray for the work of God in their lives. How could others pray for you today? Ask someone to pray specifically for you as a witness for Christ.

Notes:

_____

_____

_____

_____

_____

LIFE & STUDY TIPS
by Dr. Pokey Stanford

As a teacher or leader in the body of Christ, we are called to make disciples for Jesus Christ. However, we know that 75-90 percent of everyone who comes to know the Lord will do so through a friend or relative. That means our relationships with friends and family are our evangelism field. Any good 'evangelist' knows his or her audience. Do you know the spiritual condition of your audience, the people you are praying for, or, even, the people with whom you do life? Many do not. Take some time to take a personal inventory of those in your life and along your journey. You may be surprised at what you are missing.

NEXT STEPS

The following is called the 3-2-1 Model for Frangelism:

1. Make a list of three questions to which you absolutely need to know the answers. Then answer them thoroughly.

2. Make a list of two 'networks' of relationships where you invest most of your time.

3. Make a list of one person in each network you believe God may be angling into your path in order to hear the Good News.

Now, go to work using the 3-2-1 method to share the Good News with others. It isn't as foreign a concept as you think.

RESPONSE/SOCIAL MEDIA

Make a list of the tweets, posts or discussions you saw this week on social media about witnessing or sharing our faith in Jesus Christ that engaged your thoughts and spirit.

Any #hashtags catch your eye?

Any 'tweets of wisdom' you plan to share?

WEEK FOUR: COMMIT

We REACH to the world by raising the bar for commitment and mutual accountability to live and work as the body of Christ together.

Please take time to read the following Scripture and point your heart and soul back to God that you may hear God's Word and advance the Kingdom for Christ this week.

PRIMARY SCRIPTURE: ACTS 2:42-47

42 The believers devoted themselves to the apostles' teaching, to the community, to their shared meals, and to their prayers. 43 A sense of awe came over everyone. God performed many wonders and signs through the apostles. 44 All the believers were united and shared everything. 45 They would sell pieces of property and possessions and distribute the proceeds to everyone who needed them. 46 Every day, they met together in the temple and ate in their homes. They shared food with gladness and simplicity. 47 They praised God and demonstrated God's goodness to everyone. The Lord added daily to the community those who were being saved.

SERMON AND WORSHIP OUTLINE NOTES

Worship Songs or Hymns that Inspired Me:

_____

The Setting:

_____

The Primary Message:

_____

Sermon Outlines and Notes:

_____

_____

_____

_____

_____

What Did the Holy Spirit Say to Me Today?

_____

_____

_____

_____

SEVEN-DAY READING PLAN

Sunday	Acts 2:42-47
Monday	Psalm 37:5
Tuesday	2 Timothy 4:7
Wednesday	Proverbs 16:3
Thursday	Philippians 3:13
Friday	John 8:12
Saturday	1 Peter 2:15

REFLECTION AND STUDY QUESTIONS

Each week, we will ask four types of questions from our study together of the Scripture lesson:

A. **REACHING UP**: What does God say through God's Word about REACHing the world with the hope of Christ? (Listening) Read Acts 2:42-47.

What does it mean for the disciples to 'devote' themselves to the work of Christ? Has the meaning of that word changed?

Discuss the four areas to which the disciples 'devoted' themselves. Spend time looking at each area. Why would these areas be difficult to focus upon during our regular daily lives? How do the Scriptures inform how we might devote our own lives in these areas? Give examples of how the first community of believers put action to their faith together.

Notes:

_____

_____

_____

_____

_____

B. REACHING IN: What does it mean for us to live out God's Word as a means for building community in the body of Christ? (Understanding)

Make a list of your life's current devotions. What makes each of them important? Do they bring glory to God? Do they bring you closer in relationship to God? With God's people?

What would bring 'awe and wonder' in your faith walk to others as they watch your witness?

Notes:

_____

_____

_____

_____

_____

C. **REACHING DOWN**: What should your devotional/study life look like to faithfully build community and relationship with others? How does your devotional/study life encourage your commitment to God's will in your life? Give a specific example of each of the following expressions of living in community with the body of Christ:

    1. Working to bring glory to God through worship

    2. Doing life deeply with others

    3. Sharing my resources to make a difference in the world

    4. Growing as a learner and teacher in sharing my faith

    5. Serving as the hands and feet of Jesus in the world

    (Preparing)

What is one commitment you could make to God right now that would change the way you do life immediately? What would such a commitment say to God? To others?

Do a 'Scripture mine' whereby you list 15-20 Scriptures about living in biblical community and responding to God's will in your life. How would using these Scriptures for the next five weeks reshape your study, fellowship and serving life? Keep a journal and make notes.

Notes:
_____
_____
_____
_____
_____

D. **REACHING OUT**: What are the challenge and objective as we reach beyond the walls with God's Word for the world? (Responding)

Take time to read *Biblical Community* by Gilbert Bilezikian.

Name one or two people you could reach out to in order to pray for the work of God in their lives. How could others pray for you today? Ask someone to pray specifically for you as a witness for Christ.

Notes:

_____

_____

_____

_____

_____

LIFE & STUDY TIPS

by Dr. Pokey Stanford

As a teacher or leader in the body of Christ, we are called to live in biblical community with others. To what are you devoting your life? As you lead others, take time to ask your group where they are devoting their time, resources, skills, etc. What does this say about the community you keep? How could you effect positive change for you and your relationships to live deeply in authentic biblical community? Remember that biblical community is unsettling to some. Ask why. Be sensitive to the possible answers. As we begin to teach and learn about biblical community, we will always pull back the veils on tender places. But, across tender places is where many of the greatest opportunities rest.

NEXT STEPS

The example of the first community of Christians is a treasure to the modern church. Although we cannot live exactly as they did, we can begin to reshape some of our daily routines and habits. There are five primary routines or habits the Acts 2 community teaches us. How would you respond to the following commitments?

1. I will commit to attend worship at least 40 Sundays *(actually, I will try to attend each Sunday, but...)*
2. I will commit to joining a Sunday school class or small group to live in community with others. If I am already enrolled, I will commit to go deeper or be more faithful.
3. I will commit to share my resources through a tithe and faithful stewardship.
4. I will commit to share my faith with others who angle into my path.
5. I will commit to serve in at least one extended ministry of serving or outreach during the next year.

RESPONSE/SOCIAL MEDIA

Make a list of the tweets, posts or discussions you saw this week on social media about the Church and living in biblical community that engaged your thoughts and spirit.

Any #hashtags catch your eye?

Any 'tweets of wisdom' you plan to share?

WEEK FIVE: HEAL

We REACH to the world by seeking healing in all that we are and do as the body of Christ.

Please take time to read the following Scriptures and point your heart and soul back to God that you may hear God's Word and advance the Kingdom for Christ this week.

PRIMARY SCRIPTURES: MATTHEW 8:16-17 & MATTHEW 9:35

16 That evening people brought to Jesus many who were demon-possessed. He threw the spirits out with just a word. He healed everyone who was sick. 17 This happened so that what Isaiah the prophet said would be fulfilled: He is the one who took our illnesses and carried away our diseases. (Matthew 8:16-17)

35 Jesus traveled among all the cities and villages, teaching in their synagogues, announcing the good news of the kingdom, and healing every disease and every sickness. (Matthew 9:35)

SERMON AND WORSHIP OUTLINE NOTES

Worship Songs or Hymns that Inspired Me:

_____

The Setting:

_____

The Primary Message:

_____

Sermon Outlines and Notes:

_____

_____

_____

_____

_____

_____

What Did the Holy Spirit Say to Me Today?

_____

_____

_____

_____

SEVEN-DAY READING PLAN

Sunday			Matthew 8:16-17; 9:35

Monday			Isaiah 41:10

Tuesday			1 Peter 2:24

Wednesday		Psalm 103:2-4

Thursday		James 5:14-16

Friday			Psalm 41:3

Saturday:		Philippians 4:19

REFLECTION AND STUDY QUESTIONS

Each week, we will ask four types of questions from our study together of the Scripture lesson:

A. **REACHING UP**: What does God say through God's Word about REACHing the world with the hope of Christ? (Listening) Read Matthew 8:16-17; 9:35

The Scripture says that Jesus' ministry was to preach, teach and heal. Most are very aware of what preach and teach mean, but what about heal? How would you define healing in view of Scripture?

What are the different types of healing Scripture discusses? How does Jesus respond or interact with the differences? In Jesus' mission during His earthly ministry, why is healing linked as equally important as preaching and teaching? Name your two favorite healing stories.

Notes:

_____

_____

_____

_____

_____

B. **REACHING IN**: What does it mean for us to live out God's Word as a means for being a healing presence in the world? (Understanding)

Make a list of places you need healing today. How do these places in need of healing affect your daily walk with Christ and in the world? How would healing within these places change your life?

Why are we so hesitant to ask for healing? What is keeping you from asking? Be specific.

Notes:

_____

_____

_____

_____

_____

C. **REACHING DOWN**: What should your devotional/study life look like to faithfully seek and encourage healing throughout your life? How does your devotional/study life encourage your understanding and response to healing? Scripture mentions that healing does not happen alone—in fact, healing always connects us back to God and to others in the faith. Make a list for what you need to ask God. What other people along your journey can you count on to support your petition and request? (Preparing)

What is one commitment you could make to God right now that would begin healing in your life? What would such a commitment say to God? To others?

Do a 'Scripture mine' whereby you list 15-20 Scriptures about healing in Christ Jesus. How would using these Scriptures for the next five weeks reshape your study, fellowship and serving life? Keep a journal and make notes.

Notes:

_____

_____

_____

_____

_____

D. **REACHING OUT**: What are the challenge and objective as we reach beyond the walls with God's Word for the world? (Responding)

Take time to read *When God Disappears* by Shane Stanford.

Name one or two people you could reach out to in order to pray for the work of God in their lives. How could others pray for you today? Ask someone to pray specifically for you as a witness for Christ.

Notes:

_____

_____

_____

_____

_____

LIFE & STUDY TIPS
by Dr. Pokey Stanford

As a teacher or leader in the body of Christ, we cannot lead anyone anywhere we have never been. We cannot teach someone something we have never learned. Therefore, we cannot discuss and proclaim the healing power of Christ unless we seriously engage healing in our lives.

Take time to read *The Intercessory Life* by Dr. Maxie Dunnam. This helpful study guide provides a comprehensive look at the healing conversations and issues in our lives. Before you can teach about a life 'made whole,' take time to look at the 'loose ends' in your own life.

NEXT STEPS

Healing is more experience than words, but some words or prayers help us to stay focused and to begin again. Take your journal and make a list of the healing you need for your life. Then add a list of the healing those close to you need. Finally, make a list of healing for our communities and world.

Now, put the list in front of you and pray:

> *God, grant me the serenity to accept*
> *the things I cannot change,*
> *The courage to change the things I can,*
> *And the wisdom to know the difference.*

Reinhold Niebuhr wrote this prayer in its earliest form in 1937. Many earlier, oral versions of similar sentiment existed, but 1937 was the first written compilation. 1937 was a difficult year in our world. With Fascism on the rise and totalitarian states gaining control of much of the planet, Niebuhr wrote the prayer as a tangible response to a world in need of healing. But, he also knew that healing began with a commitment to make the world whole again. Change the heart, and our actions will follow. Indeed!

RESPONSE/SOCIAL MEDIA

Make a list of the tweets, posts or discussions you saw this week on social media about the Church and living in biblical community that engaged your thoughts and spirit.

Any #hashtags catch your eye?

Any 'tweets of wisdom' you plan to share?

A NEW START IN LIFE

Are you looking for a new start in life? Are you tired of living a life without meaning? Are you tired of running from Christ? Follow the simple but powerful process below to begin again. This is only the first step. But, this is YOUR moment to receive the grace God offers each of us through Christ and to no longer live at the mercy of a world that does not really care about you.

You're not here by accident. God loves you. He wants you to have a personal relationship with Him through Jesus, His Son. There is just one thing that separates you from God. That one thing is sin.

The Bible describes sin in many ways. Most simply, sin is our failure to measure up to God's holiness and His righteous standards. We sin by things we do, choices we make, attitudes we show and thoughts we entertain. We also sin when we fail to do right things. The Bible affirms our own experience—"there is none righteous, not even one." No matter how good we try to be, none of us does right things all the time.

People tend to divide themselves into groups—good people and bad people. But God says that every person who has ever lived is a sinner, and that any sin separates us from God. No matter how we might classify ourselves, this includes you and me. We are all sinners.

For all have sinned and come short of the glory of God. (Romans 3:23)

Many people are confused about the way to God. Some think they will be punished or rewarded according to how good they are. Some think they should make things right in their lives before they try to come to God. Others find it hard to understand how Jesus could love them when other people don't seem to. But I have great news for you! God DOES love you! More than you can ever imagine! And there's nothing you can do to make Him stop! Yes, our sins demand punishment—the punishment of death and separation from God. But, because of His great love, God sent His only Son Jesus to die for our sins.

God demonstrates His own love for us in this: While we were still sinners, Christ died for us. (Romans 5:8)

For you to come to God you have to get rid of your sin problem. But, in our own strength, not one of us can do this! You can't make yourself right with God by being a better person. Only God can rescue us from our sins. He is willing to do this not because of anything you can offer Him, but JUST BECAUSE HE LOVES YOU!

He saved us, not because of righteous things

we had done, but because of His mercy.

(Titus 3:5)

It's God's grace that allows you to come to Him—not your efforts to "clean up your life" or work your way to Heaven. You can't earn it. It's a free gift.

For it is by grace you have been saved,

through faith - and this not from yourselves, it is the

gift of God - not by works, so that no one can boast.

(Ephesians 2:8-9)

For you to come to God, the penalty for your sin must be paid. God's gift to you is His Son, Jesus, who paid the debt for you when He died on the cross.

For the wages of sin is death, but the gift of God is eternal life in Jesus Christ our Lord.
(Romans 6:23)

Jesus paid the price for your sin and mine by giving His life on a cross at a place called Calvary, just outside of the city walls of Jerusalem in ancient Israel. God brought Jesus back from the dead. He provided the way for you to have a personal relationship with Him through Jesus. When we realize how deeply our sin grieves the heart of God and how desperately we need a Savior, we are ready to receive God's offer of salvation. To admit we are sinners means turning away from our sin and selfishness and turning to follow Jesus. The biblical word for this is "repentance" —to change our thinking about how grievous sin is, so our thinking is in line with God's.

All that's left for you to do is to accept the gift that Jesus is holding out for you right now.

If you confess with your mouth, "Jesus is Lord," and believe in your heart that God raised him from the dead, you will be saved. For it is with your heart that you believe and are justified, and it is with your mouth that you confess and are saved.

(Romans 10:9-10)

God says that if you believe in His Son, Jesus, you can live forever with Him in glory.

For God so loved the world that He gave his one and only Son, that whoever believes in him shall not perish, but have eternal life.

(John 3:16)

Are you ready to accept the gift of eternal life that Jesus is offering you right now? Let's review what this commitment involves:

- I acknowledge I am a sinner in need of a Savior—this is to repent or turn away from sin.

- I believe in my heart that God raised Jesus from the dead—this is to trust that Jesus paid the full penalty for my sins.

- I confess Jesus as my Lord and my God—this is to surrender control of my life to Jesus.

- I receive Jesus as my Savior forever—this is to accept that God has done for me and in me what He promised.

If it is your sincere desire to receive Jesus into your heart as your personal Lord and Savior, then talk to God from your heart:

Here's a Suggested Prayer:

Lord Jesus, I know I am a sinner and I do not deserve eternal life. But, I believe You died and rose from the grave to make me a new creation and to prepare me to dwell in Your presence forever. Jesus, come into my life, take control of my life, forgive my sins and save me. I am now placing my trust in You alone for my salvation, and I accept Your free gift of eternal life.

If you have made this decision to follow Christ as your Lord and Savior, please let us know by emailing shanes@christchurchmemphis.org. We want to pray for you and celebrate this important first step in Christ.

However, we also want to encourage you to find a community of believers to share with on this journey. You are not meant to make this journey alone.

IN CONCLUSION

In your ongoing journey, every step will radiate the importance of prayer. So let's ask, "what does it mean to Pray Like Jesus?"

Dr. Stanford's book, *What the Prayers of Jesus Tell Us About the Heart of God*, was released in October 2015 by Abingdon Press and explores what prayer can truly mean in our everyday lives. We leave you with the following excerpt from the book:

For years, my grandfather used a phrase when describing parts of his spiritual journey. He would say, "I am how I pray." I loved the phrase from the moment I first heard it, although I really didn't appreciate its meaning until much later.

Over the course of my ministry, I have seen many examples of people who "lived as they prayed"—both from the positive and negative side. And just as my grandfather insisted, the condition of their prayer lives dictated so much of what would become of their journey.

Of course, I am chief among the suspects in this conversation. As one who has faced so many struggles in my life—hemophilia, becoming HIV-positive from medical treatment for my hemophilia, contracting Hepatitis C from meds for treatment, open heart surgery, diabetes, high blood pressure, liver damage and so on, I have been conscious of pretty much my every thought, decision and intention. And there is no better marker for the next steps of my life than how and what my prayer life points to in me.

Like everyone else, my journey looks like that of one who "is as he prays." And in order to describe or measure the ups-and-downs of my life, one only has to look at my prayer journal for an accurate timeline or map of the outcomes.

That is why I am so thankful for what I have learned in the course of this book. To know that Jesus not only agreed with my grandfather's statement but also basically lived His own life as a model or example of the truth, is humbling. I have mentioned to several friends that there are countless books on prayer and the praying life but that there are very few on the prayer life of

Jesus. I hope that will change now.

As I shared the moments of when Jesus slipped away to be alone with the Father, or when He prayed in the midst of difficult situations, or when He simply found prayer as His only solace or choice for approaching the earthly pain and sorrow His humanity encountered, I felt closer to Him than ever before. Sure, I still call Him Lord and Savior; I am in awe of His power and presence. But I have to admit, there are moments when I can see Him sitting under the tree, on the side of the hill, or around the campfire, and I almost can hear Him beckon me to sit with Him. And so I limp my ailing body and soul over to where He is, and I feel well and whole, even if only for a moment.

The prayers of Jesus are more than words. They are about the quiet places that caused even the Son of God to pause and breathe in the presence of the Father. They are also loud, victorious places where Jesus says, 'Yes, I knew they would get it!' And, finally, the prayers of Jesus are about a Son who had given everything for this mission of grace and reconciliation for

God's people. It had to be lonely and so different for Jesus, who, as Philippians 2 reminds us, had known a different existence before this. But, there, along the dusty roads and next to the lapping waters of the Sea of Galilee, we find Jesus taking the steps that we just could not take for ourselves. With all the stories that give me glimpses of Jesus' life and humanity, nothing is more powerful to me than to know that while He made the journey, He also took time away to 'stay in touch' with his Father. And, maybe even sweeter in the whole scene, is to know that they actually spent most of their time talking about you and me. How crazy cool and undeniably humbling is that.

ABOUT THE DEVELOPERS

DR. SHANE STANFORD is the Senior Pastor of Christ United Methodist Church in Memphis and the co-host of *We Believe in Memphis* (with Dr. Maxie Dunnam). Dr. Stanford is also the primary teacher and host of *You Matter*, a TV ministry airing throughout the Mid-South region. A former church planter, Dr. Stanford is the author of more than 15 books including *The Seven NEXT Words of Christ, When God Disappears, A Positive Life* and *The Five Stones* (co-authored with Brad Martin). He also co-authored the bestseller, *The Chronic Life* (co-authored with Deanna Favre).

DR. POKEY STANFORD is a former Associate Professor of Education at the University of Southern Mississippi and William Carey University. One of the youngest tenured professors in her field, Dr. Stanford taught in the areas of Curriculum/Instruction, Special Education, Assessment, Brain Based Development and Multiple Intelligence. She is the author of several journals and articles and was a national presenter for the Bureau of Education and Research. Dr. Stanford is married to Dr. Shane Stanford, and they are the parents of three daughters, Sarai Grace, Juli Anna and Emma Leigh.

Made in the USA
Columbia, SC
11 September 2017